SALARIYA

Published in Great Britain in MMXIII by
Book House, an imprint of
The Salariya Book Company Ltd
25 Marlborough Place, Brighton BN1 1UB

1 3 5 7 9 8 6 4 2

**WARNING: Fixatives should be
used only under adult supervision.**

Please visit our website at **www.salariya.com**
for **free** electronic versions of:
You Wouldn't Want to Be an Egyptian Mummy!
You Wouldn't Want to Be a Roman Gladiator!
You Wouldn't Want to be a Polar Explorer!
You Wouldn't Want to sail on a 19th-Century Whaling Ship!

Authors:
Mark Bergin was born in Hastings, England, in 1961.
He studied at Eastbourne College of Art and has
specialised in historical reconstructions as well as aviation
and maritime subjects since 1983. He lives in
Bexhill-on-Sea with his wife and three children.

David Antram was born in Brighton, England, in 1958. He studied at
Eastbourne College of Art and then worked in advertising for fifteen years
before becoming a full-time artist. He has illustrated many children's
non-fiction books.

Carolyn Franklin is a graduate of Brighton College of Art, England,
specialising in design and illustration. She has worked in animation,
advertising and children's fiction and non-fiction. She has a particular interest
in natural history and has written and illustrated many books on the subject.

Editor: Rob Walker

PB ISBN: 978-1-908759-70-2

PAPER FROM
SUSTAINABLE
FORESTS

A CIP catalogue record for this
book is available from the
British Library.

Printed and bound in China.
Printed on paper from sustainable sources.

DRAW ANIMALS

BOOK HOUSE

Contents DRAW

Drawing materials

Try using different types of drawing paper and materials. Experiment with charcoal, wax crayons and pastels. All pens, from felt—tips to ballpoints, will make interesting marks — you could also try drawing with pen and ink on wet paper.

Felt—tip

Silhouette is a style of drawing that uses only a solid black shape.

Ink

Lines drawn in **ink** cannot be erased, so keep your ink drawings sketchy and less rigid. Don't worry about mistakes as these lines can be lost in the drawing as it develops.

Hard **pencils** are greyer and soft pencils are blacker. Hard pencils are graded from 6H (the hardest) through 5H, 4H, 3H and 2H to H. Soft pencils are graded from B, 2B, 3B, 4B and 5B up to 6B (the softest).

Charcoal is very soft and can be used for big, bold drawings. Ask an adult to spray your charcoal drawings with fixative to prevent smudging.

Pastels are even softer than charcoal, and come in a wide range of colours. Ask an adult to spray your pastel drawing with fixative to prevent it from smudging.

7

DRAW
Perspective

If you look at any object from different viewpoints, you will see that the part that is closest to you looks larger, and the part furthest away from you looks smaller. Drawing in perspective is a way of creating a feeling of space — of showing three dimensions on a flat surface.

Box construction lines can help with perspective.

The vanishing point (V.P.) is the place in a perspective drawing where parallel lines appear to meet. The position of the vanishing point depends on the viewer's eye level. Sometimes a low viewpoint can give your drawing added drama.

V.P.

Two-point perspective drawing

Low eye level
(view from below)

Two-point perspective uses
two vanishing points: one for
lines running along the figure,
and one on the opposite side
for lines running across the
figure. This gives a very
realistic effect.

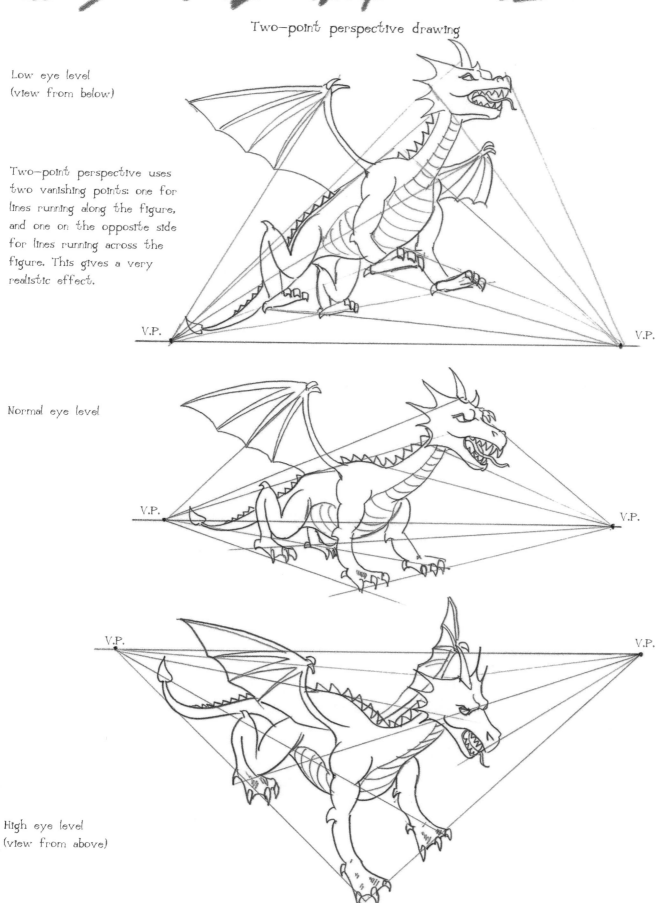

V.P.   V.P.

Normal eye level

V.P.   V.P.

V.P.   V.P.

High eye level
(view from above)

Heads, paws and claws

Pets have many different types of heads, paws and claws. Studying and sketching the detailed features of a pet will help you with your final drawings.

Quick pencil sketches can help you to understand the structure of paws and claws.

Look for areas where tone should be darker and also for changes of texture.

The more you study a subject and practise drawing it, the more accurate your drawings will become.

Try to capture as much detail
as you can in your sketches.

Look carefully at the size and
shape of the eyes, ears and nose.
Note the length of the whiskers.

Always consider the light source and
add tone to the darker areas.

Dog

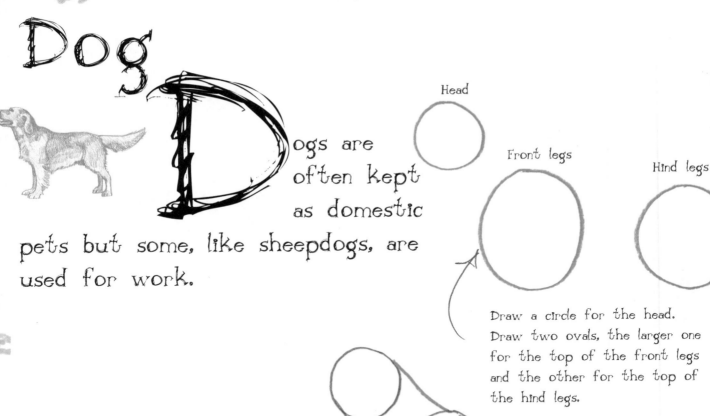

Dogs are often kept as domestic pets but some, like sheepdogs, are used for work.

Head

Front legs

Hind legs

Draw a circle for the head. Draw two ovals, the larger one for the top of the front legs and the other for the top of the hind legs.

Join the two ovals and the circle with simple lines.

Sketch in the shape of the front legs and paws.

Sketch in the basic shape of the hind legs, remembering that the top half of each leg curves outwards.

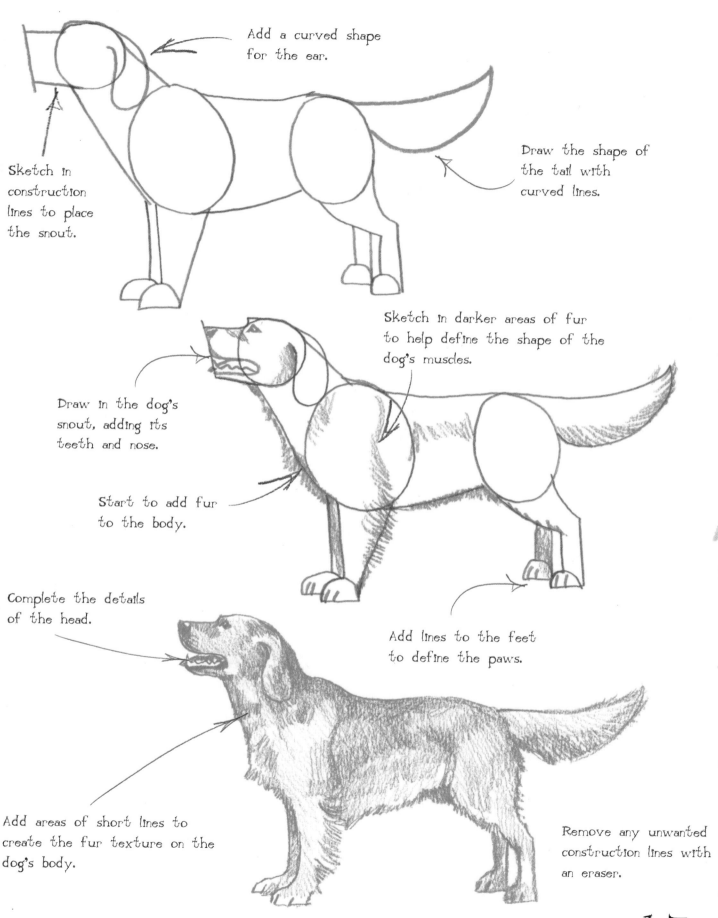

Add a curved shape for the ear.

Sketch in construction lines to place the snout.

Draw the shape of the tail with curved lines.

Sketch in darker areas of fur to help define the shape of the dog's muscles.

Draw in the dog's snout, adding its teeth and nose.

Start to add fur to the body.

Complete the details of the head.

Add lines to the feet to define the paws.

Add areas of short lines to create the fur texture on the dog's body.

Remove any unwanted construction lines with an eraser.

13

Cat

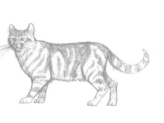

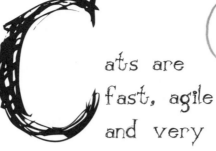ats are fast, agile and very independent animals. They are one of the most popular pets.

Head

Front legs

Hind legs

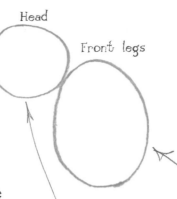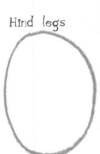

Draw a circle for the head. Draw two ovals for the top of the front legs and the top of the hind legs. The circle for the head should be touching the front oval.

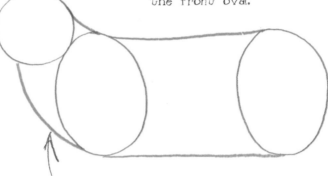

Join the ovals and the circle with simple lines.

Draw the shape of the front legs with semicircles for the paws.

Sketch the shape of the rear legs with the top halves curving outwards. Add semicircles for the paws.

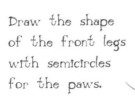

14

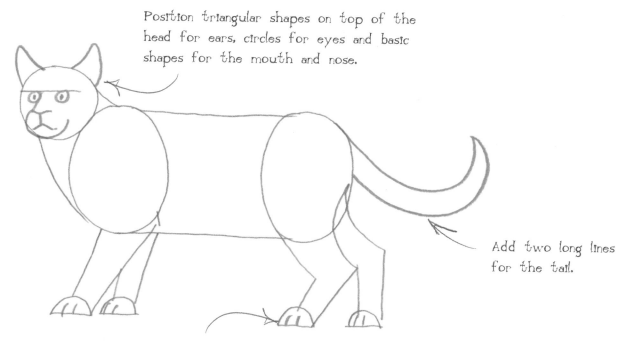

Position triangular shapes on top of the head for ears, circles for eyes and basic shapes for the mouth and nose.

Add two long lines for the tail.

Add lines to define the paws.

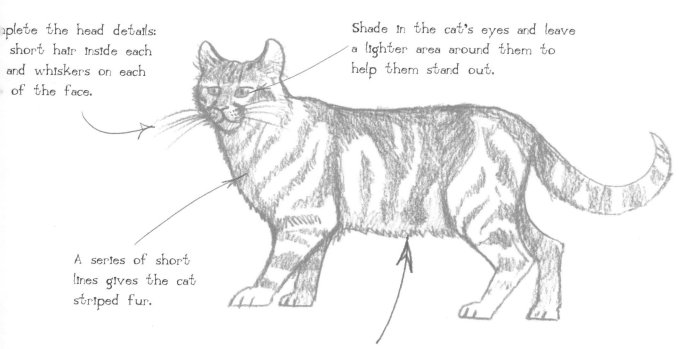

plete the head details: short hair inside each and whiskers on each of the face.

Shade in the cat's eyes and leave a lighter area around them to help them stand out.

A series of short lines gives the cat striped fur.

Add jagged lines around some edges of the cat's body to create fur.

Remove any unwanted construction lines with an eraser.

15

DRAW
Hamster

Small, furry hamsters have large cheek pouches for carrying food.

Draw a small oval and a large oval for the body.

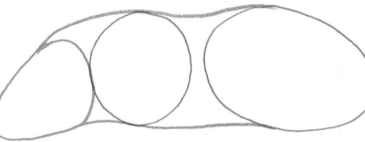

Body

Draw in the head shape touching the first oval. Join all three shapes together with curved lines.

Head

Sketch in the position of the hamster's ears, eyes, nostrils and mouth.

Add a short stubby tail.

Draw in the basic shape of the paws.

Shade in the eyes and the inside of the ears.

Add areas of tone to the body shape to suggest fur.

Remove any unwanted construction lines.

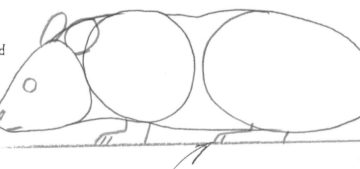

Complete the details of the paws.

Add darker shading to areas that light would not reach.

Head

Body

Draw overlapping circles and ovals for the head and body.

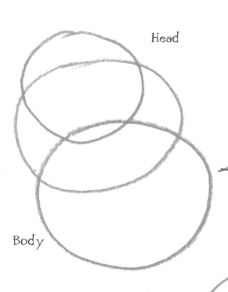

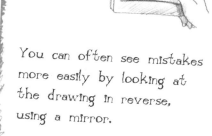

You can often see mistakes more easily by looking at the drawing in reverse, using a mirror.

Add two small ovals for paws and connect them to the body with curved lines.

Draw in the basic paw shapes.

Sketch in the position of the ears, eyes, nose and mouth.

Complete the body shape by adding curved lines.

Complete the head details by adding dark tone to the ears and the eyes.

Draw in jagged lines around the hamster for a furry texture.

Add lines to define the paws.

Leave some of the hamster's belly mostly white to suggest fur colour.

Use an eraser to remove any unwanted construction lines.

17

Rabbit

Rabbits are popular pets that are usually kept outside in a hutch.

Draw a circle for the head and two ovals for the shoulders and rear.

Head

Shoulders

Rear

Draw two long connecting curved lines.

Add two front legs using straight lines, and use half circles for the front paws.

Sketch in the basic shape of the rear legs and paws.

By framing your drawing with a square or a rectangle you can make it look completely different.

Position the rabbit's ears on its head.

Sketch in the rabbit's muzzle using straight lines.

Add a little round tail.

This drawing of a rabbit from a different angle shows all the construction lines used.

Add the head details: draw in the ears, eyes, small nose and mouth.

Add tone to the rabbit's body to give the impression of fur.

Add shading to areas where the light would not reach.

Remove any unwanted construction lines using an eraser.

Fish

Pet fish are often highly decorative

and brightly coloured.

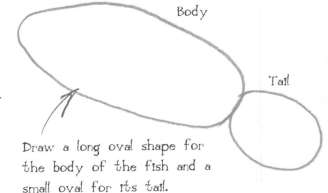

Body

Tail

Draw a long oval shape for the body of the fish and a small oval for its tail.

Add a series of curved lines for the fins.

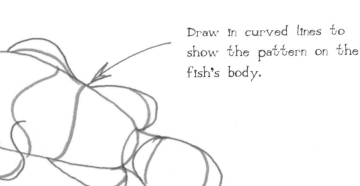

Add a small circle for the eye and put a dot in the middle.

Draw in curved lines to show the pattern on the fish's body.

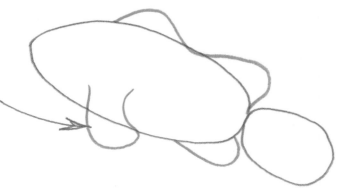

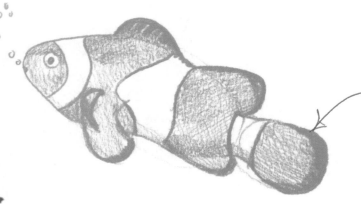

Add tone to define the pattern and to create darker areas of shading.

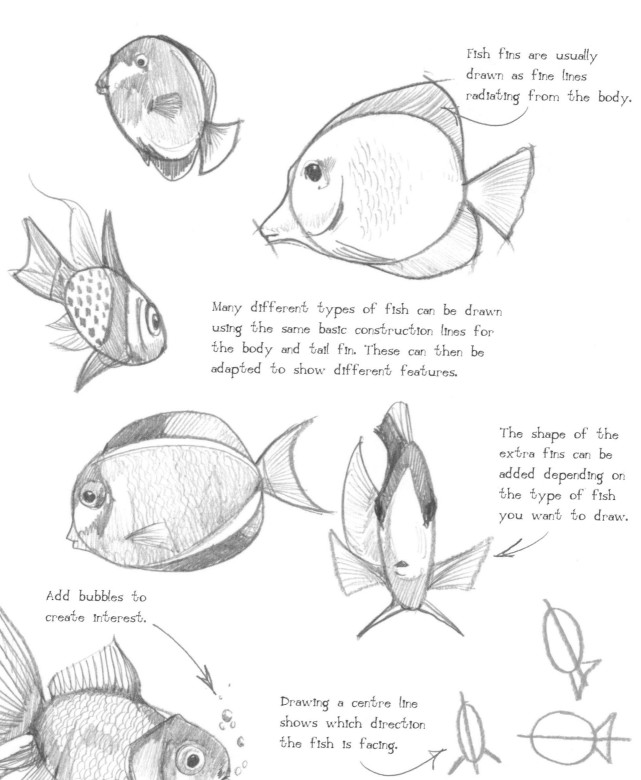

Fish fins are usually drawn as fine lines radiating from the body.

Many different types of fish can be drawn using the same basic construction lines for the body and tail fin. These can then be adapted to show different features.

The shape of the extra fins can be added depending on the type of fish you want to draw.

Add bubbles to create interest.

Drawing a centre line shows which direction the fish is facing.

Using an eraser, remove any unwanted construction lines when the drawing is finished.

21

Parrot

P arrots are large, colourful birds that can often mimic a person's speech.

Head

Body

Draw two ovals for the parrot's head and body.

Join the head to the body with two curved lines.

Draw in the shape of the tail with two long lines.

Sketch in a simple tube shape as a perch.

Draw the basic shape of the claws around the perch.

Sketch in long curved lines to add the wing shape.

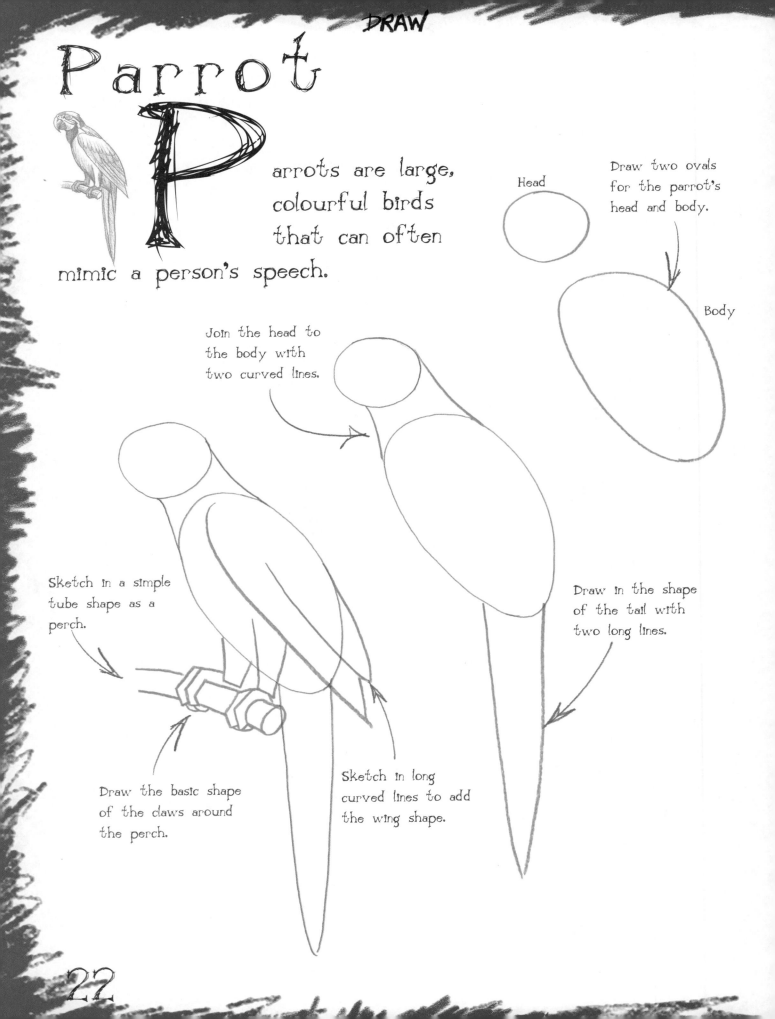

Add the eye and define the markings of the face and head.

Draw in the hook-shaped beak.

Add in layers of feathers with a series of short curved lines.

Add tone. Leave the front of the beak white to create a reflective shine.

Divide the tail into two with one long line.

Carefully add the complex feather details of the face.

Add a dark area of tone under the head.

Study different parts of the parrot. Observe how its beak shape works or how individual feathers link together.

Add lines around the claws.

Add tone to define each of the feathers.

Use an eraser to remove any unwanted construction lines.

23

Mouse

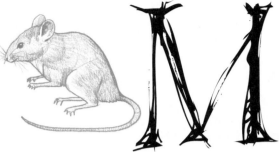

M

ice are small members of the rodent family and make good pets.

Draw three ovals, one for the head and two for the body. Connect the body shapes with a curved line.

Add in the basic shape of the front and back limbs.

Draw in the eye shape.

Sketch in rounded shapes for the ears.

Sketch in paws at the end of each limb.

Draw two long curving lines for the tail.

Add dark areas
inside the ears.

Add whiskers.

Add patches of tone to create
a fur texture. Pay attention to
the direction of the fur to make
it as realistic as possible.

Add detail
to the tail.

These three examples show how to
use the construction lines to draw a
mouse in different positions.

Mice are very
flexible. The body
can look long or
short depending on the
angle you view it from.

Fur can have many patterns and
shades, so use different depths of
tone to describe these patterns.

Remove any unwanted construction
lines using an eraser.

25

Snake

S nakes frighten many people, but to others they make great pets.

Draw one long curvy line for the snake's spine.

Add an oval for the head.

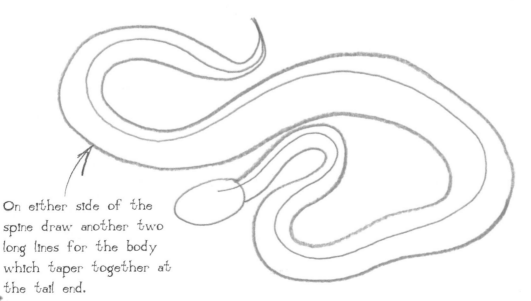

On either side of the spine draw another two long lines for the body which taper together at the tail end.

Add in the shape of the snake's head (see instructions below).

Add tone to the snake's body to give it a distinctive pattern.

Complete the head details, adding its eyes, nostrils and tongue.

Add shadow under the snake depending on the direction of the light source.

A snake's head has a distinctive shape. Create a construction—line box as shown here to help you draw the head and features.

A drawing of a snake's head from the side shows the raised areas and the positions of the features.

Use an eraser to remove any unwanted construction lines.

27

DRAW Bearded dragon

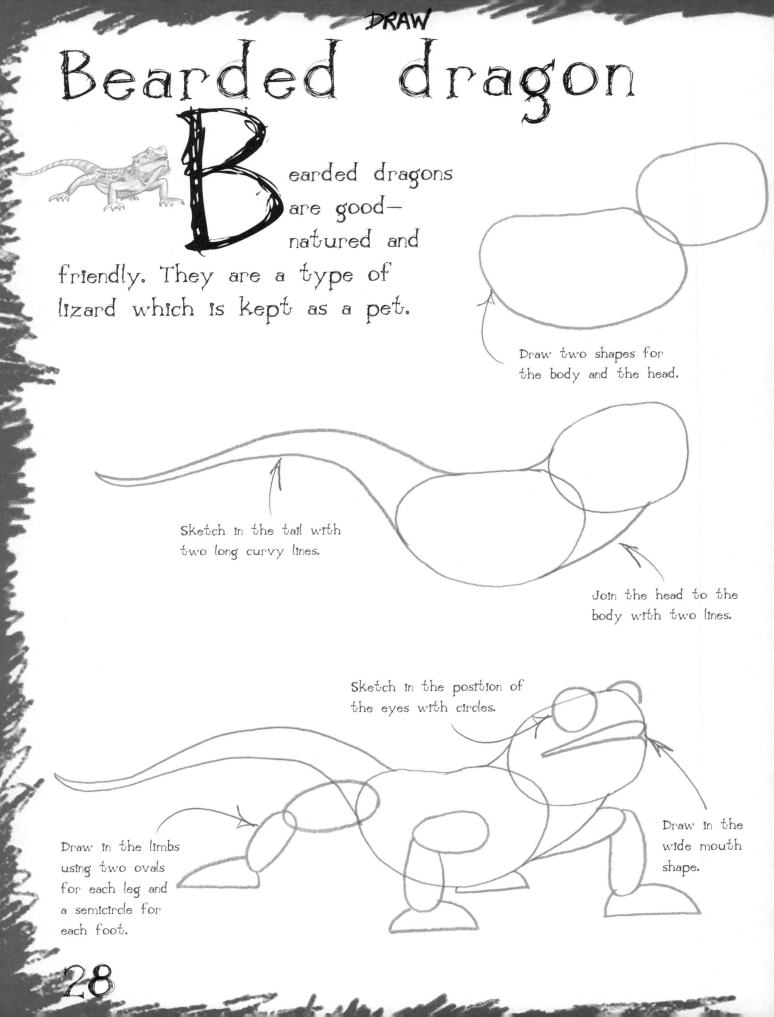

Bearded dragons are good—natured and friendly. They are a type of lizard which is kept as a pet.

Draw two shapes for the body and the head.

Sketch in the tail with two long curvy lines.

Join the head to the body with two lines.

Sketch in the position of the eyes with circles.

Draw in the limbs using two ovals for each leg and a semicircle for each foot.

Draw in the wide mouth shape.

Draw the eye in the centre of the circle.

Sketch jagged lines down the back and mid-body.

Draw in the claws on each foot.

Draw jagged lines to show the spikes fanning out from the back of the head.

Add a curved line to show the underside of the chin.

Add stripes to the tail using tone.

Add more ridges to the back.

Leave a highlighted area on top of the head to suggest its shiny scales.

Complete the sharp claws.

Add shading to any areas where light won't reach.

Complete the head details: add an ear hole at the side of the head. Darken the inside of the mouth using tone.

Remove any unwanted construction lines with an eraser.

29

Tiger

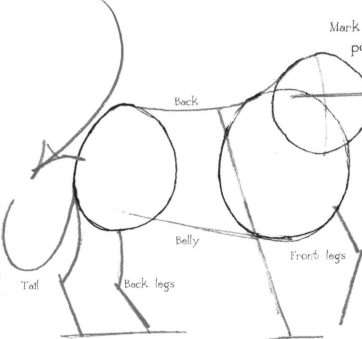

The tiger is the largest and the heaviest of the cat family. It usually hunts alone, charging after its prey from about 20 m away. A tiger kills its victim by biting the back of its neck or throat. Tigers can live for up to 26 years in the wild.

First draw circles for the head and for the front of the body.

Draw an oval for the tiger's rear end.

Rear

Head

Front body

Make a curved line for the tail.

Mark the eye position and the centre of the face.

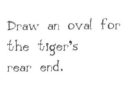

Back

Belly

Front legs

Tail

Back legs

Draw the curves of the back and the belly.

Add lines for the legs and indicate the ground they stand on.

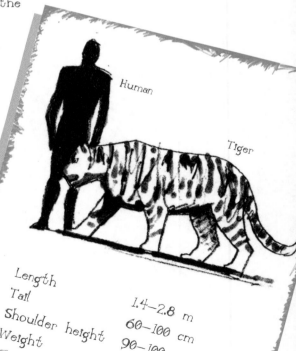

Human

Tiger

Length	
Tail	1.4–2.8 m
Shoulder height	60–100 cm
Weight	90–100 cm
	Up to 220 kg

Draw in the ears.

Draw lines for the eyes and for the position of the nose and mouth.

Finish the shape of the tail.

Nose

Mouth

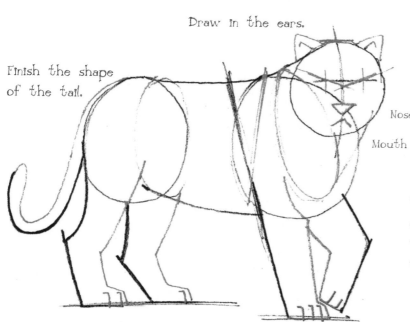

When drawing the legs and feet, imagine the tiger's body is a tube with legs set into it.

Draw the tiger's face and stripes.

Draw the stripes with a soft black pencil using marks that follow the fur's direction.

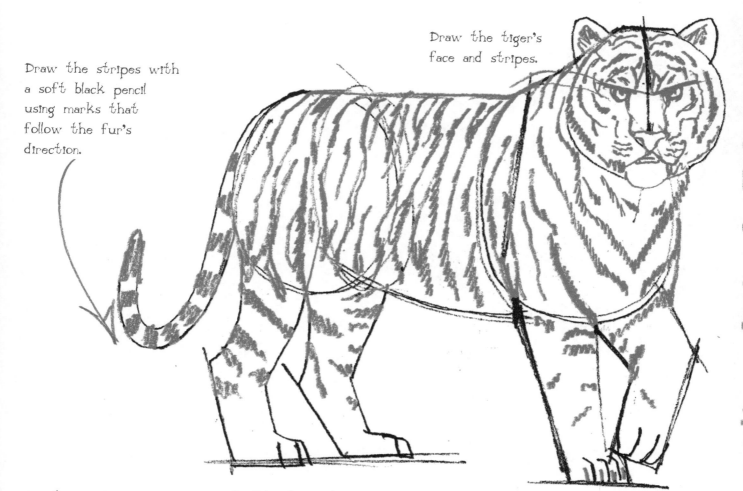

A tiger's orange and black stripes provide it with subtle camouflage in dappled light and shade.

Lion

The magnificent lion is the second largest of the big cats. Fully grown males can weigh over 230 kg and can measure over 3 m long from tail tip to nose. A lion's roar can be heard up to 8 km away and is the loudest sound made by any big cat.

Draw circles for the head, muzzle and rear and a large oval for the front of the body.

Rear

Head

Muzzle

Belly

Front

Draw lines under the belly and up to the muzzle.

Use the size of the lion's head as a unit of measurement to help keep your drawing in proportion. The lion is 3 heads tall and its body is 3.5 heads long.

Mark out the eye line and the sides of the muzzle.

Back

Mane

Add lines for the position of the legs and the lion's feet. Draw lines for the back and tail.

Tail

Legs

Sketch in circles for the lion's mane and ears.

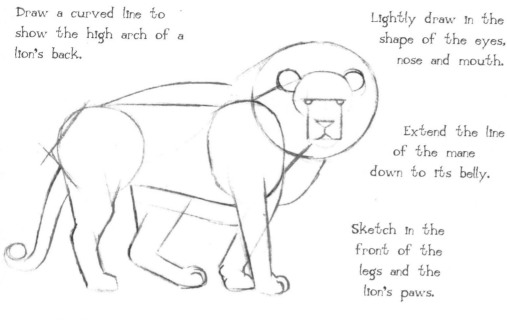

Draw a curved line to show the high arch of a lion's back.

Lightly draw in the shape of the eyes, nose and mouth.

Extend the line of the mane down to its belly.

Sketch in the front of the legs and the lion's paws.

Make the lion's hindquarters more angular.

Finish drawing in the eyes, nose and mouth.

Draw the lion's mane using your pencil marks to follow the direction of the hair.

Finish drawing the hindquarters. Shade in the muscles.

A mane can make a lion appear larger, which scares away other male lions.

33

DRAW Panther

A panther is a leopard or a jaguar with a black coat. Panthers are found in dense, dark tropical rainforests where their colouring camouflages them well for hunting.

When drawing a dark object, look to see which direction the light is coming from. Draw in the darkest parts of your subject first. Slowly build up the grey areas leaving some white paper showing through as the lightest parts of your drawing.

Draw circles for the head, front and rear of the body.

Back

Head

Rear

Belly

Front

Put in lines for the back and belly.

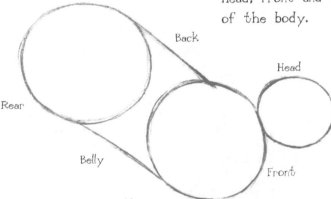

Tail

Indicate the panther's eye position and draw a circle for its muzzle.

Neck

Sketch in a long curved tail.

Eyes

Muzzle

Back legs

Draw in curved and straight lines for the back legs and feet.

Front legs

Add lines for its neck, front legs and feet.

Add the back and
front of the neck.

Ears

Draw in the
ears, nose and
mouth.

Finish drawing the
tail. Sketch in the
curve of the back
and belly.

Back legs

Belly

Draw the front of
the legs and the shape
of the paws.

Front legs

Paws

Round off any sharp
corners. Shade in the
light and dark areas of
fur (as explained
opposite).

Finish drawing the
panther's face and ears.

Stand the panther firmly
on the ground so he is
not floating!

Panthers often attack from
behind, dragging their prey
up into trees to eat later.

DRAW Tiger's head

An average male tiger stands 90 cm tall at shoulder height. Unlike other members of the cat family, tigers are not good tree climbers. However, they are strong swimmers and in floods they are known to swim in search of stranded prey.

Draw a circle for the head and an oval for the muzzle.

Head

Back of the neck

Muzzle

Front of the neck

Add lines for the front and back of the neck.

Highlight

Shadow

Eyes are often the focal point of a drawing. Study and sketch the eyes of different animals. Look at the highlight on the eye and at the shape of the pupil.

Look carefully at the angle of the ears and draw them in. Indicate the eye positions.

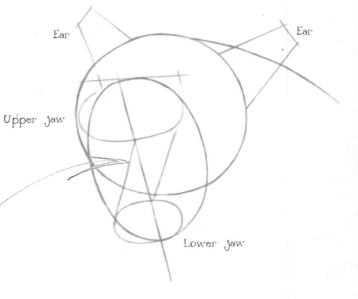

Ear

Ear

Upper Jaw

Lower Jaw

Draw two ovals, one for the lower jaw and the other for the upper jaw.

Draw two lines to join the lower jaw to the back of the mouth.

The maximum lifespan of a tiger is usually around 26 years and for most of their lives, tigers live alone.

Draw in the fur on either side of its face.

Draw in the large front teeth (top and bottom).

Draw the tiger's gums and the position of its back teeth.

Draw the screwed-up face and eyes of the tiger.

Sketch in the shape of the tiger's stripes. Block in the areas of grey tone first, and then the areas of dark tone.

Lastly, use a fine paintbrush and white paint for the paler whiskers.

DRAW Leopard

Leopards are agile climbers and often haul their prey into the branches of a tree. They hunt alone and mainly at night. Each leopard has its own territory that it defends from other leopards.

Draw circles for the leopard's rear end, head and muzzle.

Rear

Head

Front leg

Muzzle

Sketch in the curve of the neck and back and the line of the front leg.

Draw the long curved line of the tail.

Tail

Back leg

Paw

Add straight lines for the back leg, and draw circles for the paws.

Draw a circle for one ear, and a triangle for the other.

Ears

Mark the position of the eyes and the muzzle.

Paw

Make the leg shapes rounded to show the muscles in the legs, and finish the paws.

Sketch in the neck line and the side of the face. Lightly draw in the eyes and nose. Add the lower jaw.

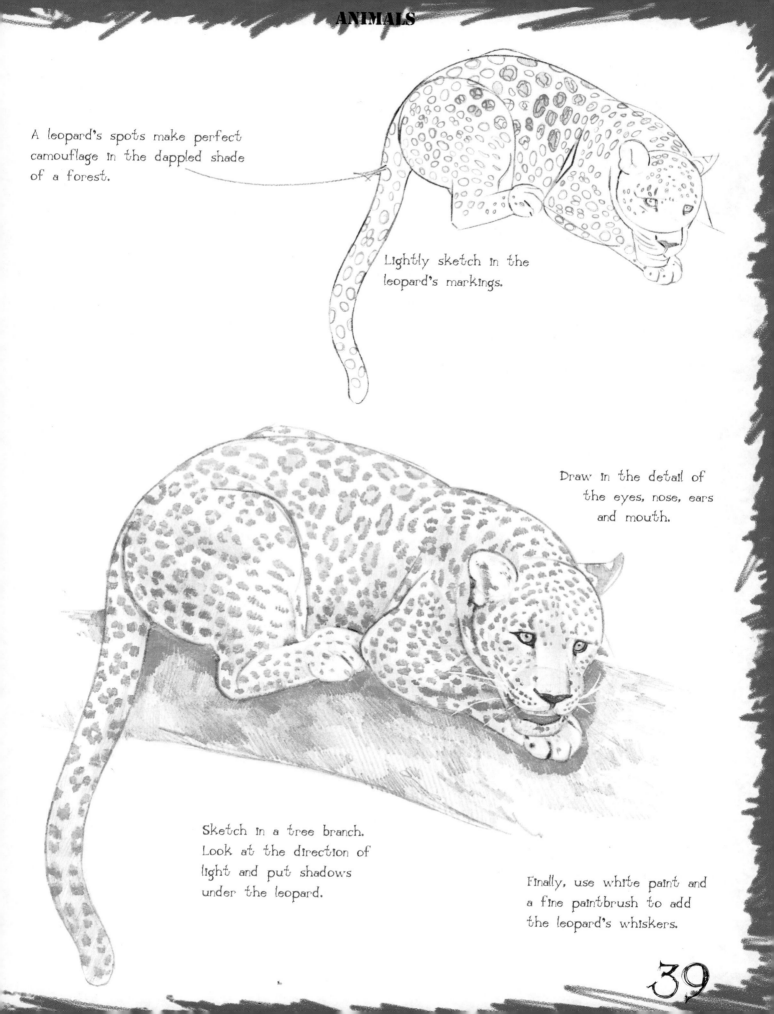

A leopard's spots make perfect camouflage in the dappled shade of a forest.

Lightly sketch in the leopard's markings.

Draw in the detail of the eyes, nose, ears and mouth.

Sketch in a tree branch. Look at the direction of light and put shadows under the leopard.

Finally, use white paint and a fine paintbrush to add the leopard's whiskers.

Lynx

ynx are smaller than many other big cats. They live alone, mainly in pine forests, high up on mountain slopes. A lynx has a stubby tail, long tufted ears, a short body and large feet.

Study these drawings of a polar bear and a brown bear. Compare ear and muzzle shapes. Check the position of their features. Using construction lines helps create three—dimensional looking drawings.

Draw circles for the head, front and rear ends of the lynx.

Front

Head

Rear

Sketch in the curve of the back and tail.

Back

Tail

Lightly mark a cross at the centre of the head.

Put in straight lines for the back legs.

Back legs

Draw lines for the front legs and add circles for the paws.

Front legs

Paws

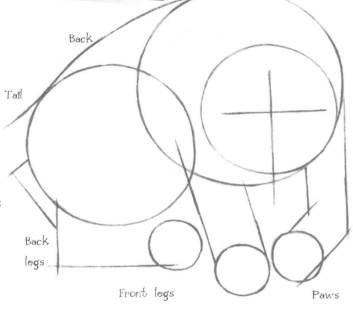

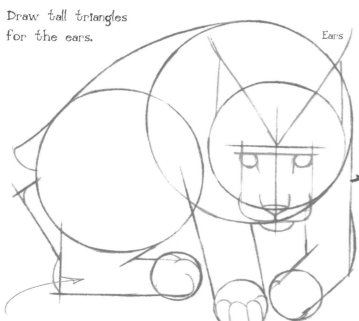

Draw tall triangles for the ears.

Ears

Draw the eyes just below the centre line. Draw lines down for the direction of the muzzle.

Sketch in the nose, and the upper and lower jaws.

Complete the tail and paws. Round off the back legs.

Draw the ears with their distinctive tufts. Finish off the eyes and the face.

A lynx will follow the scent trail of its prey for many kilometres.

Sketch in the lynx's markings. Draw the areas of mid—tone first, then add the dark tone.

41

Cheetah DRAW

The cheetah is the world's fastest land animal. It can run up to 96 kph. It hunts mainly in the early morning or twilight. Its preferred prey is either a Thompson's gazelle or an impala.

To smudge small areas of a drawing you need to make a paper cone. Place the tip of your pencil into the centre of the cone and gently rub at the lines. Use your finger to smudge larger areas. Ask an adult to spray finished drawings with fixative to prevent further smudging.

Draw circles for the head, front and rear end of the cheetah.

Add lines for its back and belly and indicate its neck.

Back

Head

Neck

Rear

Belly

Front

Draw in the long curved line of the tail.

Draw in the muzzle.

Draw in the lines for the legs. See how they make a triangular shape under the cheetah's body.

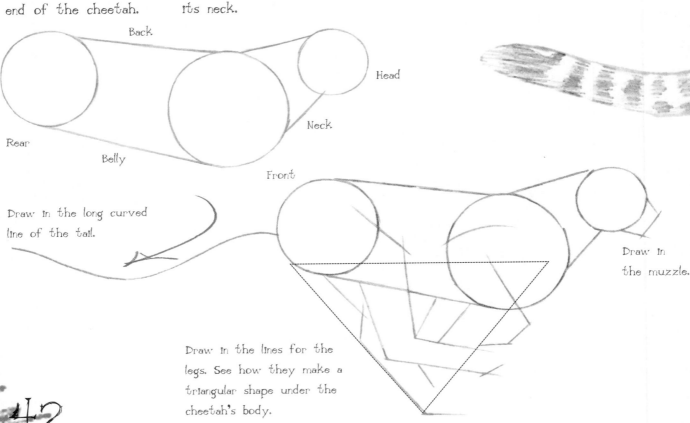

Finish the tail. It acts as a counterbalance to the rest of the cheetah's body.

Draw the ears and mane.

Curve the lines of the cheetah's back and belly.

Sketch in the eye, nose and mouth.

A cheetah has a streamlined body and a small head. Its long legs and flexible spine give the cheetah the maximum length of stride necessary for great speed.

Finish the legs and sketch in the paws. Round off all sharp angles.

Draw the cheetah's spotted coat. The tail markings begin as spots but gradually become stripes.

Draw in the face markings.

To give the impression of speed, carefully smudge both hind legs. (The drawing should still show through.)

43

DRAW
Lion cubs

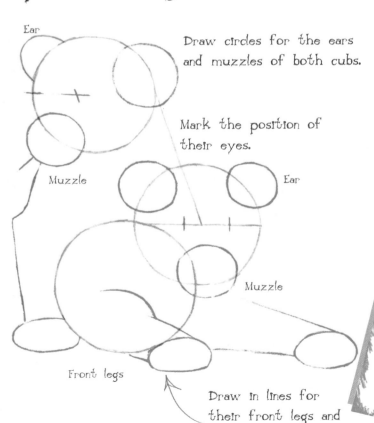

Lions live in family groups called prides. Each pride consists of several females, their cubs and at least one male. Lion cubs start learning to hunt at about 11 months old but cannot catch prey until they are nearly 16 months old. A cub weighs about 1.3 kg at birth and up to 230 kg when adult.

Draw a circle for the head of the top cub and a line for its neck. Mark in its eye level.

Head

Neck

Head

Draw two circles for the head and body of the lower cub. Mark in its eye level.

Body of right cub

Draw circles for the ears and muzzles of both cubs.

Mark the position of their eyes.

Ear

Ear

Muzzle

Muzzle

Front legs

Draw in lines for their front legs and ovals for paws.

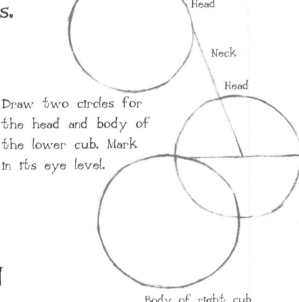

An important part of creating a good drawing is your composition. Use a small cardboard frame of the same proportion as your drawing paper, to help you judge your composition. Hold the frame in front of your subject and more it around to try different views.

44

Study each cub's expression before drawing their eyes. Draw in each cub's nose and mouth.

Sketch in the ears. Finish drawing the paws and the front legs. Draw in the top cub's neck.

Put dark tones on the faces.

Puma

The puma is highly adaptable and makes its home in habitats as diverse as lowland prairies, forests or high mountains. Its territory can cover many kilometres and it hunts both day and night.

Sketch in circles for the puma's head, chest, shoulders and rear end.

Draw curved lines for the back and belly. Draw the puma's neck.

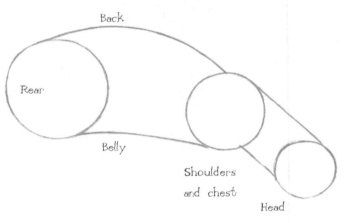

Back

Rear

Belly

Shoulders and chest

Head

Draw the front and back legs. Draw circles for paws.

Shoulder

Tree trunk

Back legs

Front legs

Sketch the tree trunk and branches.

Draw curved lines for the side of the puma's face and neck.

Tail

Draw the puma's long curved tail. Draw in the toes and round off any sharp angles.

Sketch in the eyes and muzzle. Add triangles for the ears.

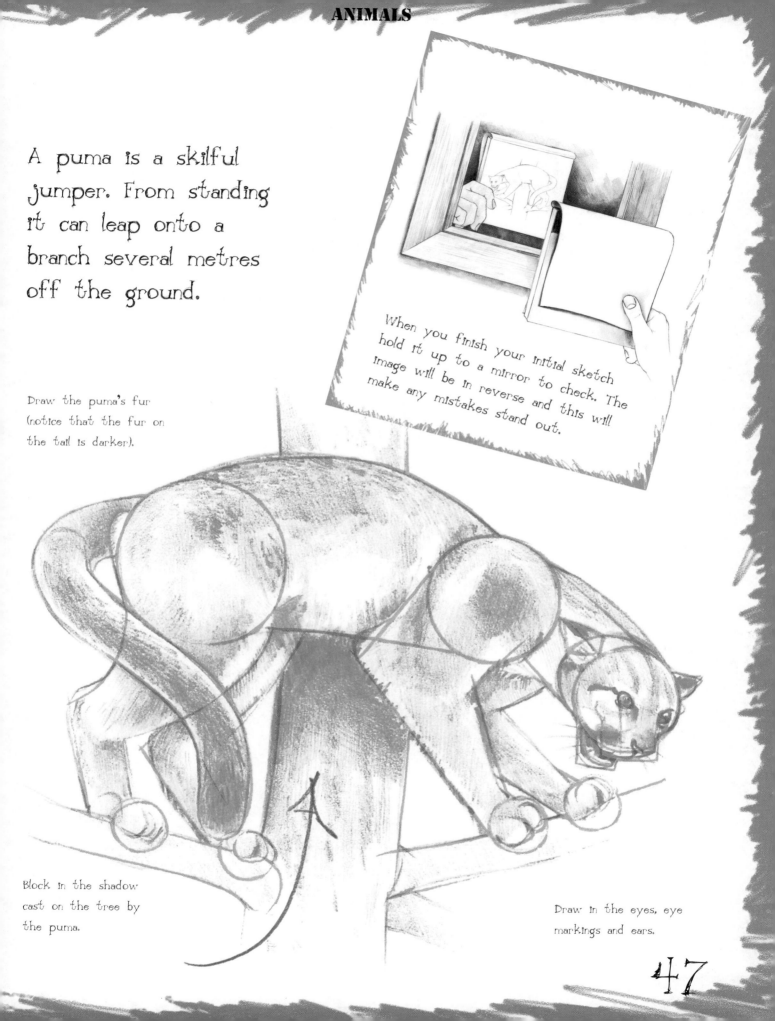

A puma is a skilful jumper. From standing it can leap onto a branch several metres off the ground.

When you finish your initial sketch hold it up to a mirror to check. The image will be in reverse and this will make any mistakes stand out.

Draw the puma's fur (notice that the fur on the tail is darker).

Block in the shadow cast on the tree by the puma.

Draw in the eyes, eye markings and ears.

47

Horse

Horses are large, fast—running mammals. They have four long legs and hoofed feet.

Draw two circles for the head. Make one smaller than the other.

Draw two circles for the body.

Draw two curved lines to form the neck.

Draw the shape of the head with two straight lines.

Sketch two curved lines, one for the back and one for the belly.

Draw four small circles for the knees and four more for the fetlocks.

Sketch the front and back legs and hooves.

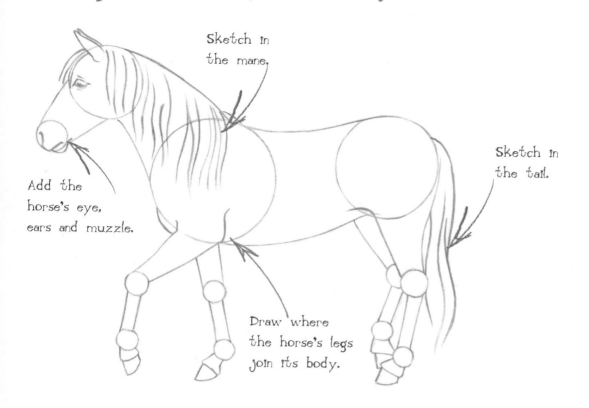

Sketch in
the mane.

Sketch in
the tail.

Add the
horse's eye,
ears and muzzle.

Draw where
the horse's legs
join its body.

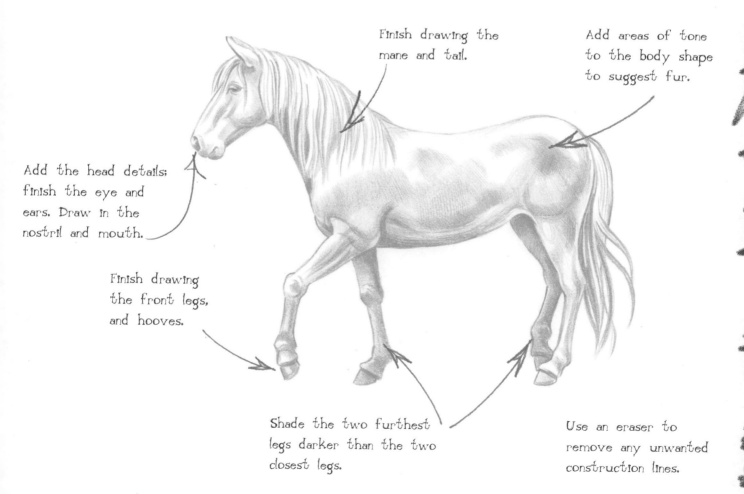

Finish drawing the
mane and tail.

Add areas of tone
to the body shape
to suggest fur.

Add the head details;
finish the eye and
ears. Draw in the
nostril and mouth.

Finish drawing
the front legs,
and hooves.

Shade the two furthest
legs darker than the two
closest legs.

Use an eraser to
remove any unwanted
construction lines.

DRAW Macrauchenia

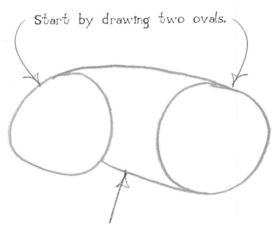

This weird—
looking herd
creature is
found in fossils from South
America and lived about
7 million to 20,000 years ago.
Charles Darwin found the first
fossil of this animal on his
voyage aboard the *Beagle*.

Start by drawing two ovals.

Add two curved lines to
connect the ovals.

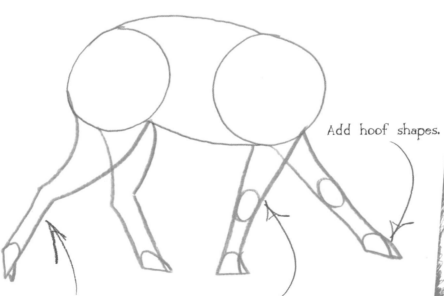

Add hoof shapes.

Add the back legs. They
have curved lines at the
top, switching to straight
lines for the lower half.

Sketch in the shape of
the front legs, adding a
circle at the joints.

Paying particular attention to
the key characteristics can
help your drawing work.
Specific shapes such as the
head and hooves / feet can
define an animal.

Draw an oval for the head.

Position the eye and ears.

Add two curved lines for a neck to connect the head to the body.

Indicate the jaw line.

Add the small trunk—like nose.

Add curved lines for the tail.

Complete the details of the head.

Add dark tone running up the back of the Macrauchenia to show its markings.

Use the construction lines as a guide to add muscle structure.

Add a mountainous background with trees and grass.

Add darker tone to areas where light would not reach.

Soften some of the lines to create a fur texture.

Remove any unwanted construction lines.

51

DRAW
Andrewsarchus

The Andrewsarchus was perhaps the largest carnivorous mammal ever to live. It stood around 1.8 metres tall and was about 5.2 metres long.

Draw a curved line for the spine.

Start by sketching in two ovals of different sizes for the front and rear haunches.

Construction lines should always be drawn lightly. That way you can easily erase them when you finish the drawing.

Draw in construction lines to position the head.

Add simple shapes for the front legs. One leg should bend.

Add the back legs. Use curved lines for the upper part.

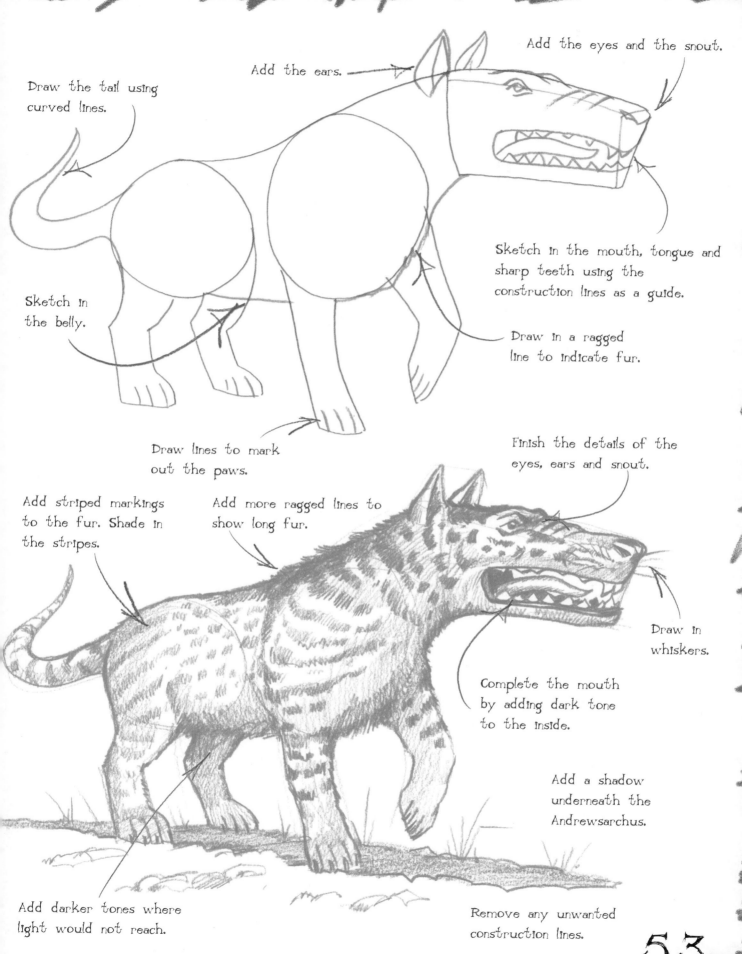

Draw the tail using curved lines.

Add the ears.

Add the eyes and the snout.

Sketch in the mouth, tongue and sharp teeth using the construction lines as a guide.

Sketch in the belly.

Draw in a ragged line to indicate fur.

Draw lines to mark out the paws.

Finish the details of the eyes, ears and snout.

Add striped markings to the fur. Shade in the stripes.

Add more ragged lines to show long fur.

Draw in whiskers.

Complete the mouth by adding dark tone to the inside.

Add a shadow underneath the Andrewsarchus.

Add darker tones where light would not reach.

Remove any unwanted construction lines.

53

Basilosaurus

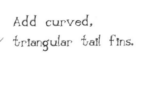

The Basilosaurus was a **gigantic** carnivorous whale—like creature. Fossils of this giant creature, measuring 18 metres in length, have been found in Louisiana, Egypt and the Sahara desert.

Add an oval for the head.

Start by drawing a large bean shape for the body.

Add curved, triangular tail fins.

Draw in the tail using long, curved lines.

Add the eyes.

Sketch in the jagged sharp teeth.

Add small fins to the body.

Add two large flippers.

Add tone to the back. Keep your pencil lines in the same direction to create the skin effects.

Try looking at your drawing in a mirror. Seeing it in reverse can help you spot mistakes.

Finish the detail of the head.

Leave white areas along the body to show the sheen of the skin.

Remove any unwanted construction lines.

Add some prey for the Basilosaurus.

55

DRAW
Indricotherium

Indricotherium lived around 30 to 25 million years ago. This large land mammal would have eaten the tallest parts of trees in the same way as a giraffe.

Draw two large ovals for the body. Add a line at the top for the spine.

Draw in the thick back legs.

Add a curved underbelly.

Draw in the front legs, overlapping them to indicate that one leg is behind the other.

Add two long, curved lines for the thick neck.

Sketch in the eyes, nose and ears.

Use curving lines to show the shape of the head.

Draw in curved lines around the body to suggest muscle structure.

Draw in small semicircles for the toes.

Add tone to define the shape of the head.

Add a long, curvy tail.

Add lots of lines to indicate the leathery skin folds of the body.

Add bristles at the end of the tail.

Shade in areas where light wouldn't reach.

Remove any unwanted construction lines.

Add in the ground.

DRAW Phorusrhacos

Phorusrhacos is known as one of the 'terror birds'. It stood 3 metres tall and fed on small mammals and carcasses.

Draw an oval for the head.

Draw a curved line for the neck.

Draw a larger oval for the body.

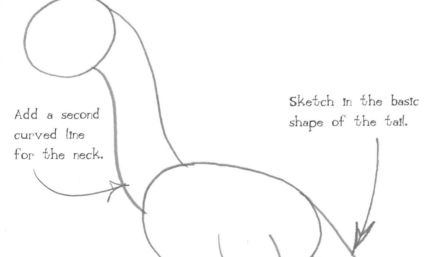

Add a second curved line for the neck.

Sketch in the basic shape of the tail.

Draw in the legs with long, curved lines.

Add construction lines to position the base of the feet.

By framing your drawing with a square or a rectangle you can make it look completely different.

Sketch in the shape of the curving beak and position the eye.

Sketch in construction lines for the head plumage.

Using the construction lines as a guide, draw in the feather shapes of the head plumage.

Add another line to the neck.

Add a jagged line for where the feathers overlap the leg.

Add lots of curved lines for the feathered plumage.

Add tone to the beak and finish the head details.

Shade areas where light wouldn't reach.

Add toes and talons to the feet.

Add lines to create skin texture.

Sketch tonal stripes onto the legs.

Add the ground.

Remove any unwanted construction lines.

Woolly rhino
DRAW

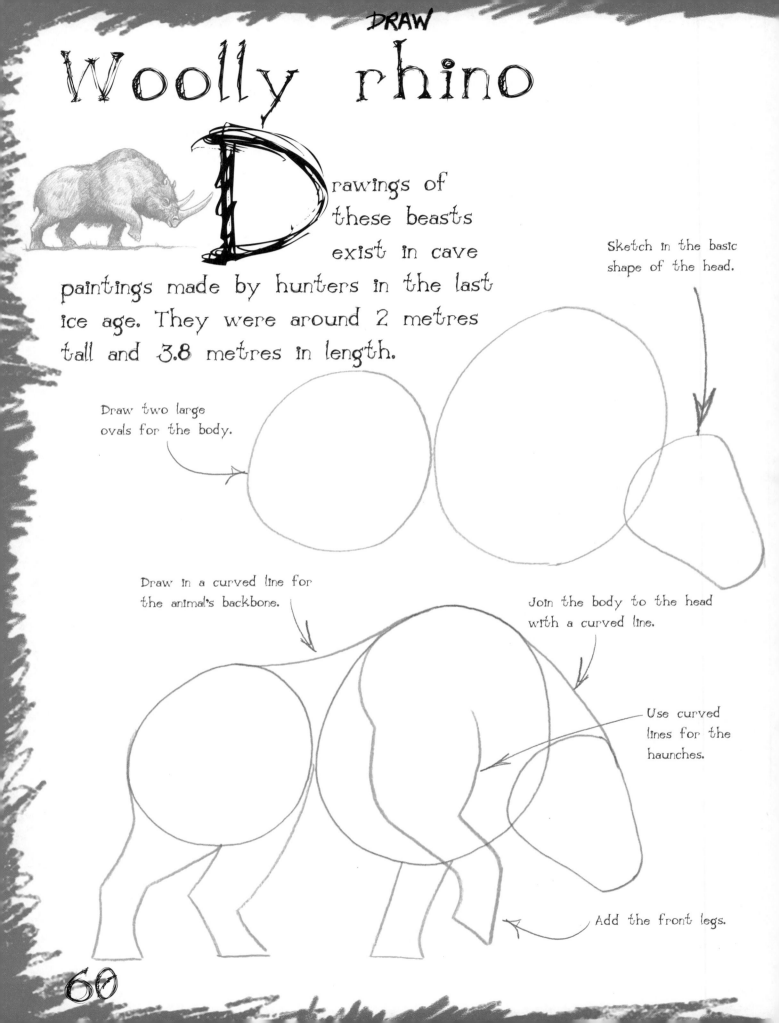

Drawings of these beasts exist in cave paintings made by hunters in the last ice age. They were around 2 metres tall and 3.8 metres in length.

Sketch in the basic shape of the head.

Draw two large ovals for the body.

Draw in a curved line for the animal's backbone.

Join the body to the head with a curved line.

Use curved lines for the haunches.

Add the front legs.

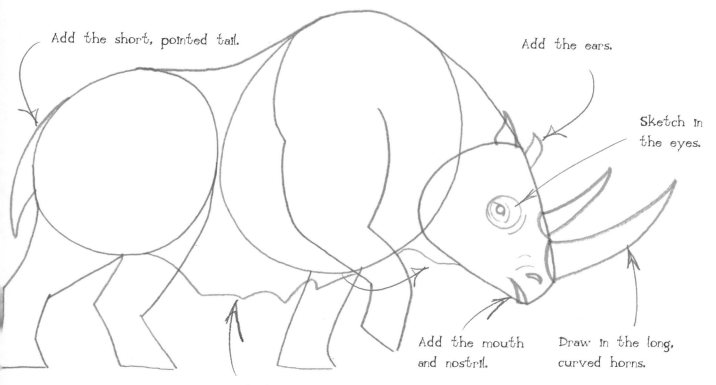

Add the short, pointed tail.

Add the ears.

Sketch in the eyes.

Add the mouth and nostril.

Draw in the long, curved horns.

Draw a jagged shape to indicate the woolly underbelly.

Draw the woolly coat using lots of short lines. Make the lines denser where you want to show shade and tone.

Add dense fur lines along the spine.

Complete the head details. Note how the fur direction changes. Add dark areas to the eye, mouth and nostril.

Sketch in coarse fur on the underbelly.

Add shading to the underside of the horns.

Add the ground.

Add darker tone to areas light wouldn't reach.

Remove any unwanted construction lines.

DRAW Megatherium

This giant ground sloth stood 6 metres high and weighed around 3.8 tonnes! It lived 1.9 million to 80,000 years ago.

Add dark shading to parts of your drawing for a dramatic effect. Artists call this chiaroscuro.

Draw two large ovals for the body.

Add a curved line for the spine.

Sketch in the basic shape of the head.

Add a curved line for the neck.

Draw a long curved line for the belly.

Use curved lines to draw in the legs.

Add long, pointed toes.

Add the eye, nostril, ear and downturned mouth.

Sketch a jagged line around the outline to indicate fur.

Sketch in the arms with long, pointed fingers.

Finish drawing the head details.

Draw in the fur using lots of short lines. Vary the frequency for areas of light and dark.

Sketch in a curved tail.

Use many short lines to define the arms.

Draw in a tree and shrubbery for added effect.

Add shading to where light won't reach.

Remove any unwanted construction lines.

63

DRAW Smilodon

This large sabre—tooth cat hunted grazing animals, pinned them down with its powerful front legs and killed them with its bite. Males could reach 3 metres in height.

Start by drawing two ovals.

Join the two ovals with a curved line for the spine.

Add two curved lines for the neck to join the head to the body.

Always check the negative space — the area around your drawing. This can help you spot mistakes.

Sketch in the shape of the head.

Add a line for the belly.

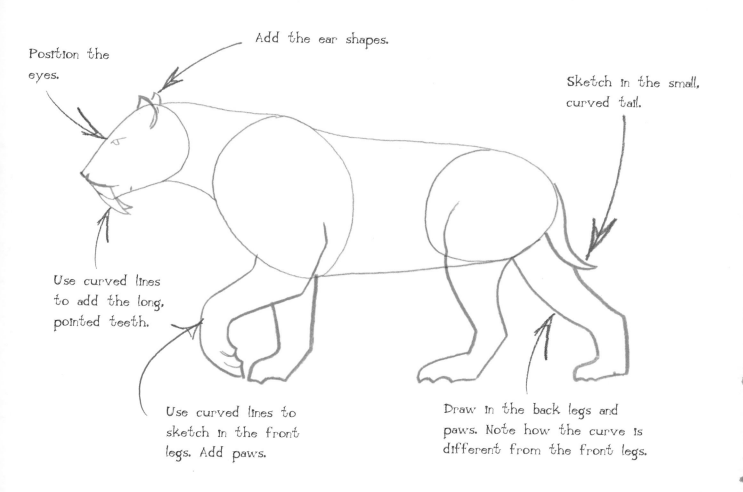

Position the eyes.

Add the ear shapes.

Sketch in the small, curved tail.

Use curved lines to add the long, pointed teeth.

Use curved lines to sketch in the front legs. Add paws.

Draw in the back legs and paws. Note how the curve is different from the front legs.

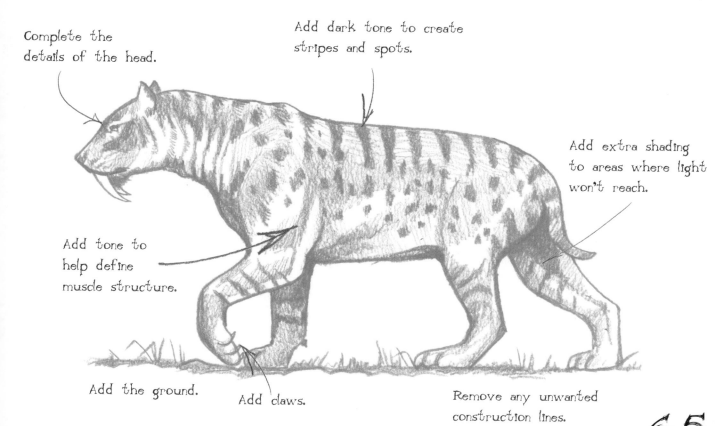

Complete the details of the head.

Add dark tone to create stripes and spots.

Add extra shading to areas where light won't reach.

Add tone to help define muscle structure.

Add the ground.

Add claws.

Remove any unwanted construction lines.

65

Woolly mammoth

These giants of the ice age grazed on vegetation. Males could grow to a height of 3 metres. Bones and frozen carcasses have been found from Ireland to Siberia in Russia and also throughout Europe.

Start by drawing three overlapping ovals.

Add curved lines to link the three ovals together.

Draw in long, curved lines to add the thick front legs.

Note how the back legs curve differently from the front legs.

66

Sketch in an eye and an ear.

Sketch long, curved lines for the trunk.

Add long, curved lines for the tusks.

Add a line for the tail.

Add a dark, coarse patch of hair on top of the mammoth's head.

Darken the areas around the eye and ear.

Draw in lots of short lines for the mammoth's fur. Vary the frequency to create areas of light and dark.

Vary the fur length and make some areas more coarse and straggly.

Add dark tone to areas where light would not reach.

Add a line of tone to the tusks for a three-dimensional effect.

Add the ground.

Remove any unwanted construction lines.

Centaur

A centaur is half horse, half man. Centaurs were said to have come from the mountains of Thessaly in Greece, and were wild, lawless and savage. The Greek hero Heracles killed centaurs with poison—tipped arrows.

Draw in a rectangle for the centaur's chest.

Man body

Draw two circles to form the body.

Draw in centre line

Draw in lines for the back and the belly.

Horse body

Draw the ground the centaur stands on.

Draw a line for the spear.

Head

Spear

Draw a small circle for a head and two lines to form a neck.

Arm

Add lines for the legs and arms, with circles for the joints, hands and hooves.

Front legs

Back legs

68

Indicate the positions of the eyes, nose and mouth.

Draw in the muscles of the upper body.

Add detail to the centaur's hands.

Add hair to the centaur's head.

Draw in the muscles of the lower body, and curved lines to show the position of the tail.

Draw in the detail of the spear.

Finish drawing in the eyes, nose and mouth.

Shade in the muscles.

Pencil lines should follow the direction of the tail.

Take a look at real horses' legs.

Use squares or rectangles to frame your composition. This can make all the difference.

Dragon

Dragons are thought to have magical and spiritual powers, and are common to many cultures of the world. These cunning creatures typically have scaly bodies, wings and fiery breath. The Chinese consider them symbols of good luck.

Draw a circle to form the head, and a larger oval for the main body.

Head

Add two lines to indicate the neck.

Main body

Sketch in shapes for the top of the head and the lower jaw.

Draw in lines for the wing base and circles for the joints.

Add a long curved line to show the position of the tail.

Head

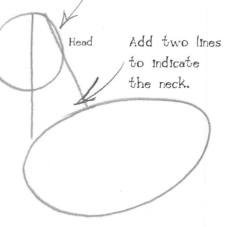

The use of light and dark to create bold images is called chiaroscura. Try this on the dragon to get more impact.

Draw triangular shapes to indicate the positions of the feet.

Add lines for front and rear legs, with circles for the joints.

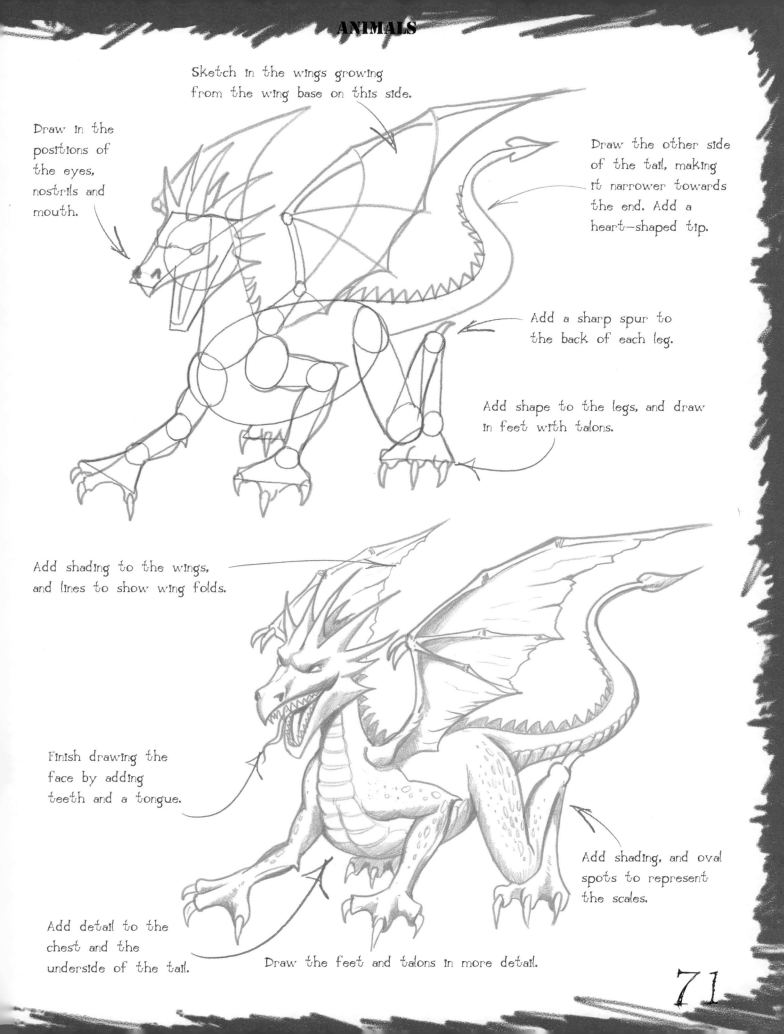

Sketch in the wings growing from the wing base on this side.

Draw in the positions of the eyes, nostrils and mouth.

Draw the other side of the tail, making it narrower towards the end. Add a heart–shaped tip.

Add a sharp spur to the back of each leg.

Add shape to the legs, and draw in feet with talons.

Add shading to the wings, and lines to show wing folds.

Finish drawing the face by adding teeth and a tongue.

Add shading, and oval spots to represent the scales.

Add detail to the chest and the underside of the tail.

Draw the feet and talons in more detail.

71

DRAW Gryphon

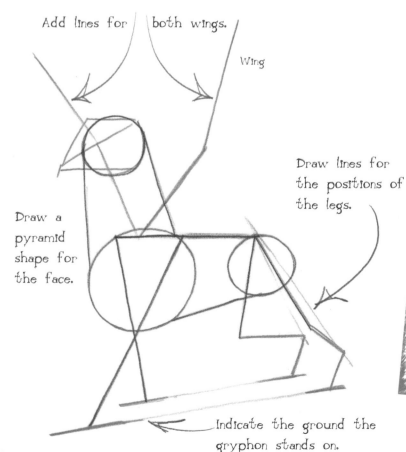

The gryphon (griffin) or lion—eagle was considered to be the king of the air, and was a powerful and majestic creature. In Persian culture, gryphons are shown drawing the sun across the sky.

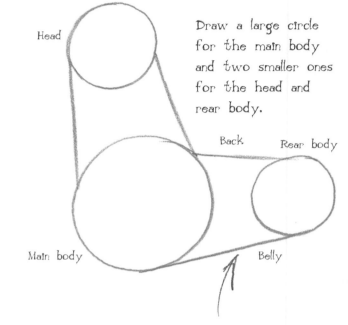

Head

Main body

Back

Rear body

Belly

Draw a large circle for the main body and two smaller ones for the head and rear body.

Draw in lines for the neck and for the back and belly.

Add lines for both wings.

Wing

Draw a pyramid shape for the face.

Draw lines for the positions of the legs.

Indicate the ground the gryphon stands on.

Look at the spaces between parts of the figure (negative space) to help check the proportions and shape of your drawing.

Wing construction

First draw two straight lines.

Add two oval shapes.

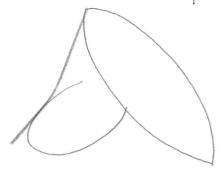

Add muscles to the wing.

Indicate the groups of feathers.

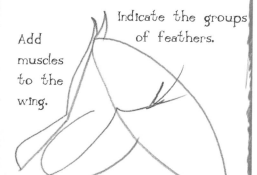

Carefully draw in rows of feathers.

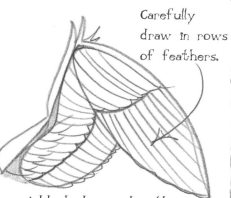

Add shading under the front edge of the wing.

Carefully sketch in the beak, then add ears and eyes.

Draw in a shield-like shape at the base of the body.

Tail

Add a curved, lion-like tail.

Add detail of back feet and legs.

Sketch in the front feet.

Finish drawing the detail of the gryphon's head.

Use short downward strokes to draw the chest feathers.

Add wing features (see left).

Add shading.

Add hair to the tip of the tail.

Draw the sharp eagle's talons.

Hydra

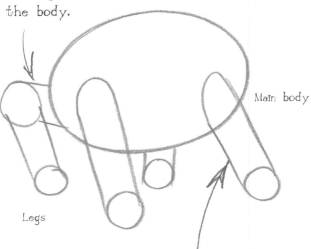

The Hydra in Greek mythology was said to guard the entrance to the underworld beneath the waters of Lake Lerna. Heracles killed this hideous creature as one of his twelve labours.

Add two lines to join this leg to the body.

Draw a large oval for the main body.

Main body

Legs

Draw four tube shapes for the legs.

Draw a circle for each of the Hydra's 9 heads.

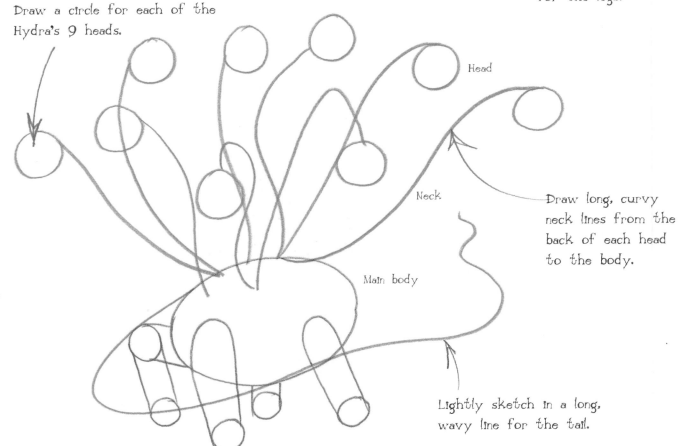

Head

Neck

Main body

Draw long, curvy neck lines from the back of each head to the body.

Lightly sketch in a long, wavy line for the tail.

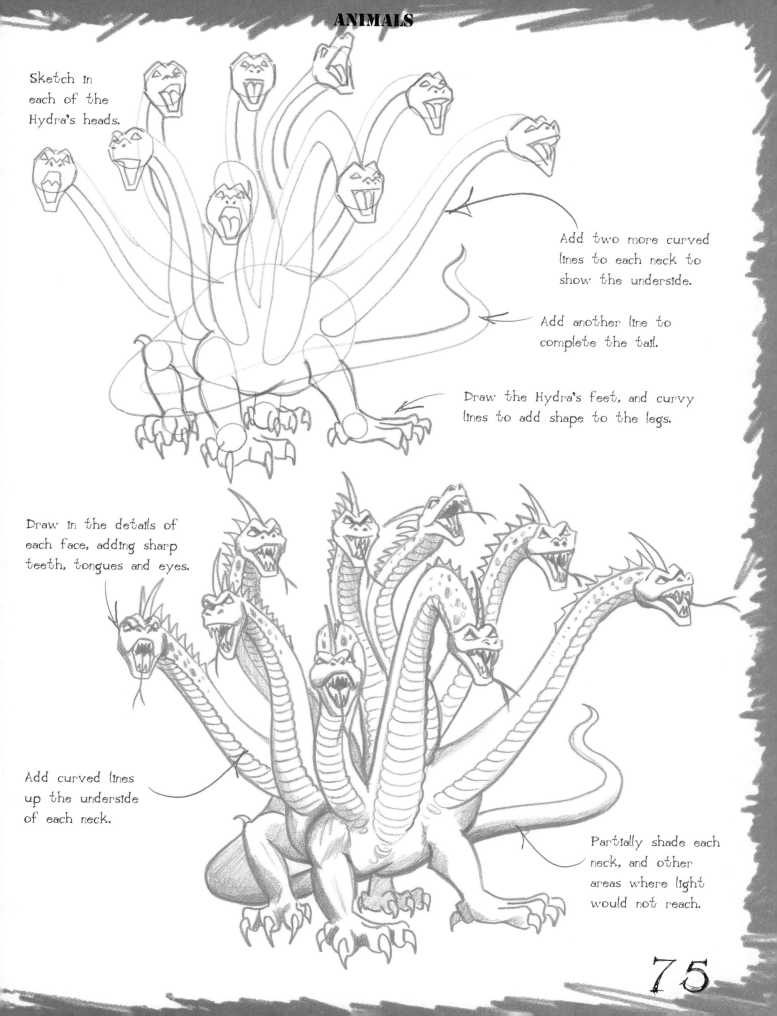

Sketch in each of the Hydra's heads.

Add two more curved lines to each neck to show the underside.

Add another line to complete the tail.

Draw the Hydra's feet, and curvy lines to add shape to the legs.

Draw in the details of each face, adding sharp teeth, tongues and eyes.

Add curved lines up the underside of each neck.

Partially shade each neck, and other areas where light would not reach.

Minotaur

The Minotaur was half man, half bull. This creature of Greek myth was said to dwell in the labyrinth constructed by King Minos at Knossos. Theseus eventually killed the beast, then found his way out safely by following the trail of string he had left to guide him.

Draw a vertical line through the centre.

Head

Sketch in two circles and an oval to form the head, main body and hips.

Main body

Hips

Centre line

Centre line

Head

Draw a line to indicate the top of the shoulders.

Arms

Sketch two ovals, one smaller and overlapping the other, to show the right arm bent at the elbow. Add a circle for the hand.

Draw a straight line passing through the hand shapes for the axe haft.

Hips

Sketch a long oval shape with a roundish oval below it to show the foreshortening of the left arm. Add a smaller overlapping circle for the hand.

Thigh

Draw a large oval for each thigh. Add two lines to join these to smaller ovals which form the lower legs. Add circles at the end of each leg for ankles, and sketch in the hooves with two semicircles.

Lower leg

Ankle

Hoof

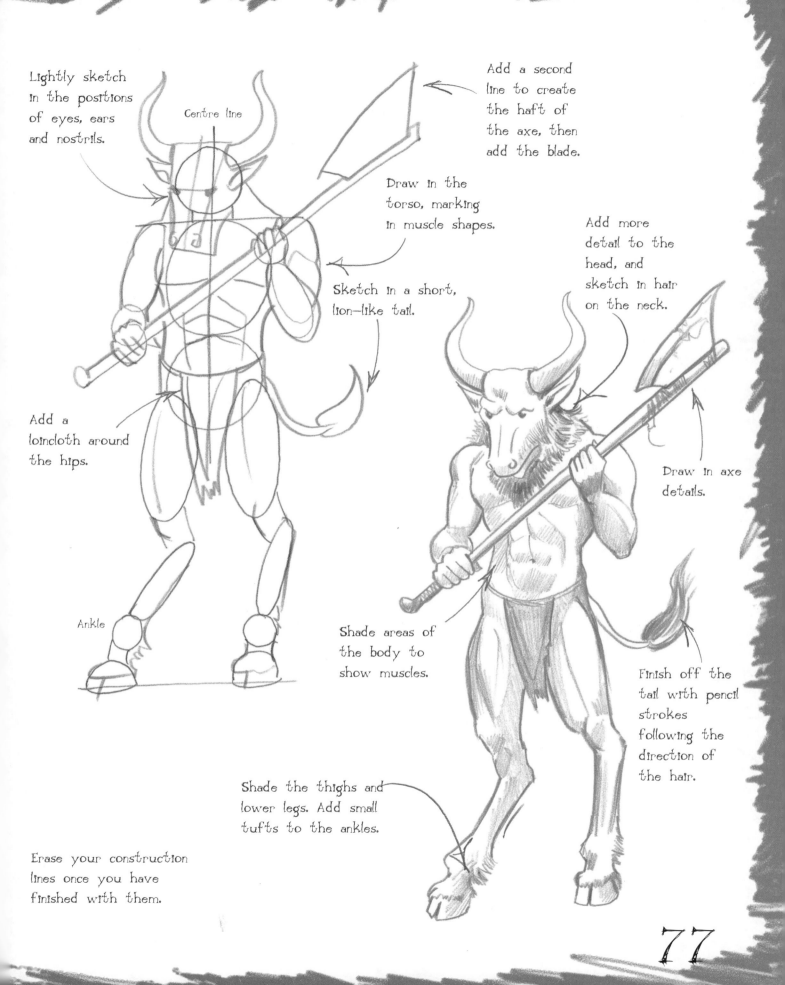

Lightly sketch in the positions of eyes, ears and nostrils.

Centre line

Add a second line to create the haft of the axe, then add the blade.

Draw in the torso, marking in muscle shapes.

Add more detail to the head, and sketch in hair on the neck.

Sketch in a short, lion-like tail.

Add a loincloth around the hips.

Draw in axe details.

Ankle

Shade areas of the body to show muscles.

Finish off the tail with pencil strokes following the direction of the hair.

Shade the thighs and lower legs. Add small tufts to the ankles.

Erase your construction lines once you have finished with them.

Pegasus

Pegasus, the Greek winged horse, was said to have been born from the blood spilt by Medusa's murder. Pegasus aided the Greek hero Bellerophon against the Chimera and the Amazons. He also brought thunderbolts to Zeus, the king of the gods.

Draw a triangle shape for the neck and a circle for the head.

Head

Back

Rear

Belly

Draw two circles, one slightly larger than the other, for the body. Add lines for the back and belly.

Draw three lines from the head and another line across to form the muzzle.

Draw a crooked line to indicate the front wing base.

Sketch in a V-shaped line to show the base of the neck.

Draw lines for the directions of the front and back legs.

To keep the object you are drawing in proportion, choose a unit of measurement that you can relate back to. Here the width of Pegasus has been divided into three. You can also mark key points in the drawing to take measurements from.

Wings

Draw a bent line for the front of the wing.

Draw a simple curved shape for the main part.

Add the inner part of the wing.

Indicate the rows of feathers.

Neatly draw in the overlapping feathers.

Sketch in the horse's eyes, mouth, nostrils and ears. Add a mane.

Draw in wing shapes.

Indicate the flowing tail.

Draw in more lines to give the legs shape. Add circles for joints.

Add more detail to the horse's head.

Draw small wing feathers first, then longer feathers.

Shade in the muscle shape.

Add more detail to the tail.

Shade in the underside of Pegasus to create a three-dimensional effect.

79

Phoenix

The phoenix is a mythical bird said to live for up to 1,461 years. It has red and gold plumage. Each time it nears the end of its life, the phoenix builds a nest of cinnamon twigs that ignites. Both the bird and its nest are turned into ashes, from which a new phoenix arises.

Draw a vertical line to mark the centre of the phoenix.

Sketch a small circle for the head.

Draw a large oval for the body.

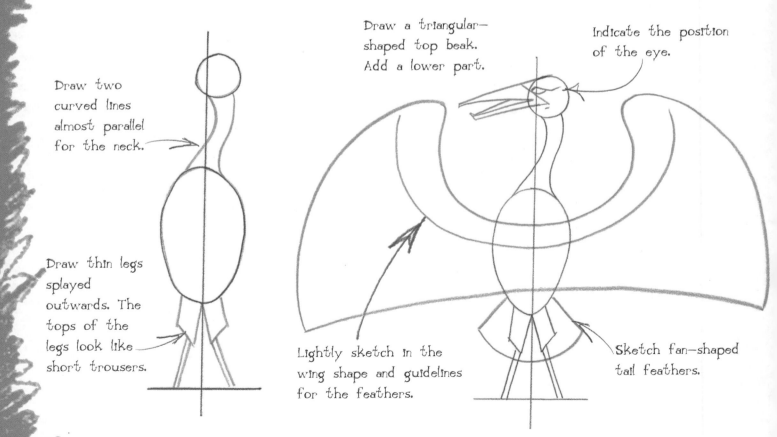

Draw two curved lines almost parallel for the neck.

Draw thin legs splayed outwards. The tops of the legs look like short trousers.

Draw a triangular-shaped top beak. Add a lower part.

Indicate the position of the eye.

Lightly sketch in the wing shape and guidelines for the feathers.

Sketch fan-shaped tail feathers.

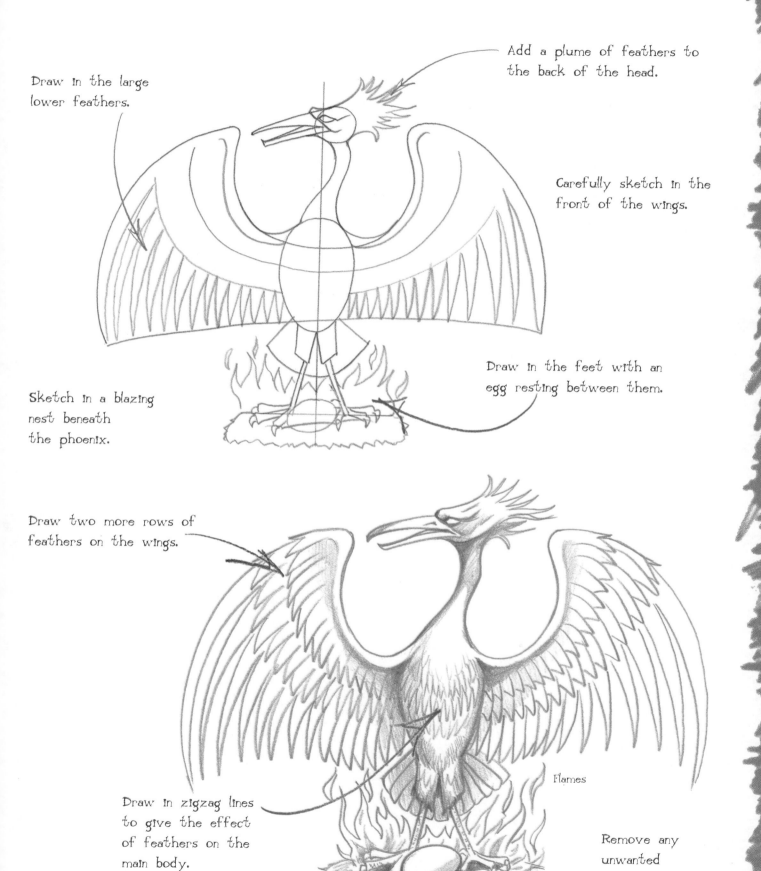

Draw in the large lower feathers.

Add a plume of feathers to the back of the head.

Carefully sketch in the front of the wings.

Draw in the feet with an egg resting between them.

Sketch in a blazing nest beneath the phoenix.

Draw two more rows of feathers on the wings.

Draw in zigzag lines to give the effect of feathers on the main body.

Flames

Remove any unwanted construction lines.

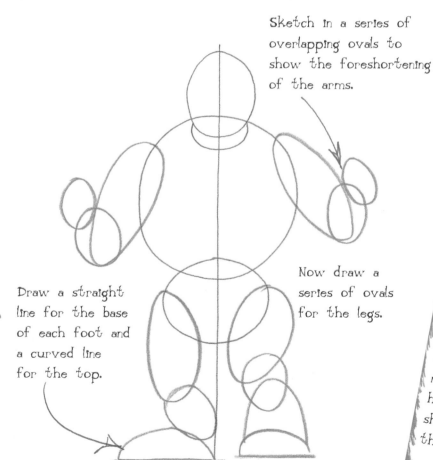

Troll

The large mountain troll features in many folk tales. They are said to be foul-smelling creatures that are dim-witted but powerful. Trolls are aggressive towards humans and carry a crude, primitive club as a weapon.

First draw a centre line.

Head

Body

Hips

Draw a large circle for the body. Draw two smaller circles overlapping at top and bottom for the head and hips.

Sketch in a series of overlapping ovals to show the foreshortening of the arms.

Now draw a series of ovals for the legs.

Draw a straight line for the base of each foot and a curved line for the top.

To draw a face, first draw a line down the centre of the head, then two horizontal lines to help you construct the face. The top horizontal line shows the position of the eyes, the top of the nose and where the ears join the head. The bottom horizontal line shows the base of the nose and the bottom of the ears.

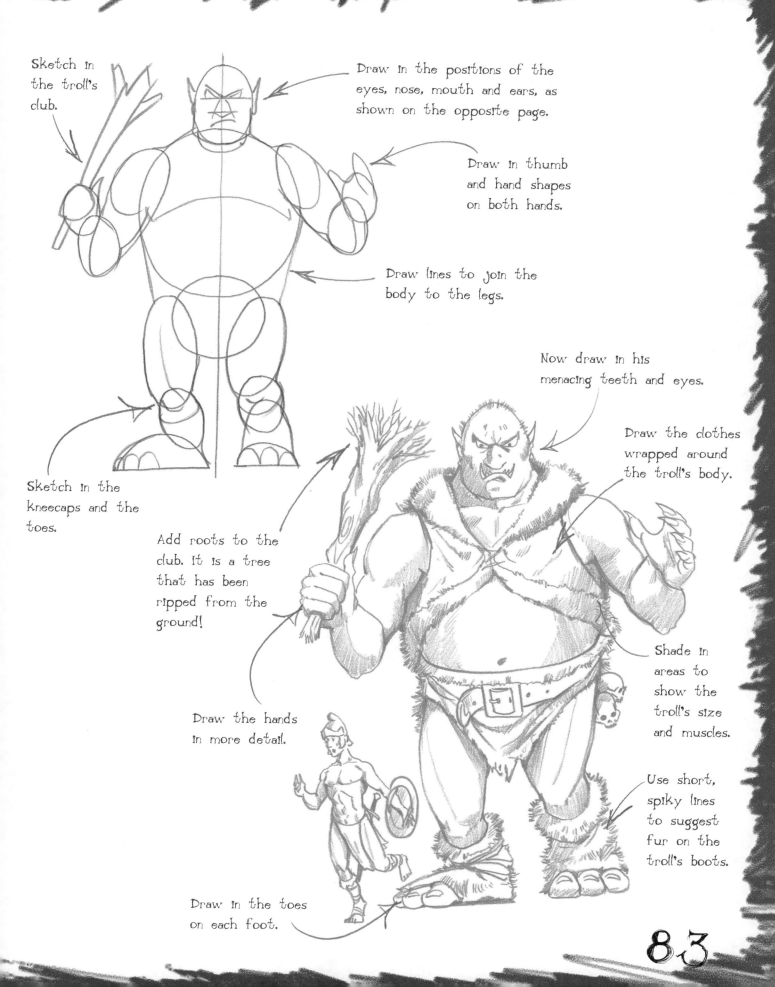

Sketch in the troll's club.

Draw in the positions of the eyes, nose, mouth and ears, as shown on the opposite page.

Draw in thumb and hand shapes on both hands.

Draw lines to join the body to the legs.

Now draw in his menacing teeth and eyes.

Draw the clothes wrapped around the troll's body.

Sketch in the kneecaps and the toes.

Add roots to the club. It is a tree that has been ripped from the ground!

Shade in areas to show the troll's size and muscles.

Draw the hands in more detail.

Use short, spiky lines to suggest fur on the troll's boots.

Draw in the toes on each foot.

Unicorn

The unicorn is a fabulous horse with a twisted horn on its head. It is said to be fierce yet good, a selfless, solitary but always beautiful creature. The ancient Greeks thought that unicorns lived in India.

Above the body, draw a circle for the head, and two lines to form the neck.

Head

Back

Rear

Front

Belly

First draw two circles, one slightly larger than the other. Draw in lines for the back and the belly.

Sketch in the muzzle by drawing a smaller circle and then joining it to the head with two lines.

Add ears.

Curved lines around the body and the base of the neck make your drawing look more three-dimensional.

Draw in the legs, using circles to show the positions of the joints.

Curve the belly line upwards.

Hold your picture up to a mirror to look at its reflection. This will help you see any mistakes in your drawing.

The hooves are semicircles.

Make your construction lines curved to show the unicorn's muscle structure.

Sketch in the eyes, nostrils and horn. Add the unicorn's mane.

Draw more detail on the unicorn's horn.

Sketch in the shape of the tail.

The mane is drawn using random jagged shapes flowing backwards.

Add more detail to the head.

Draw in the tail hair with curved lines flowing backwards.

Add detail and shading to the hooves. Leave some areas white as highlights.

Shade in areas where light does not reach to give a three-dimensional look.

Rats

Animals like rats make great cartoon characters. You can give them personalities and expressions, just as you can with cartoon people.

Start your drawing by sketching in simple shapes.

Head

Sketch an oval for the head, with a line for the top of the nose.

Body

Tail

Feet

Add a line for the tail.

Use lines for the limbs, with dots to indicate joints.

Sketch a small oval for the top of the body, then a larger one for the lower part of the body.

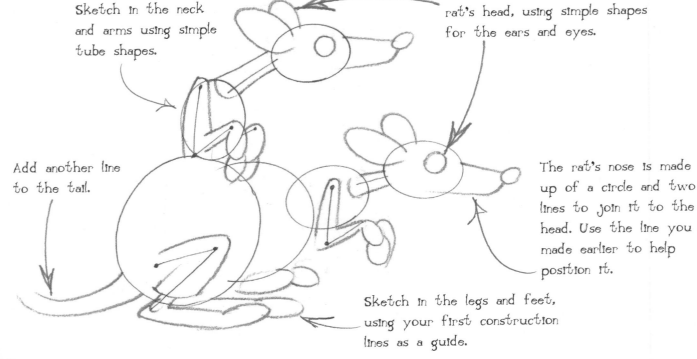

Sketch in the neck and arms using simple tube shapes.

Add the main features to the rat's head, using simple shapes for the ears and eyes.

Add another line to the tail.

The rat's nose is made up of a circle and two lines to join it to the head. Use the line you made earlier to help position it.

Sketch in the legs and feet, using your first construction lines as a guide.

Use simple curved lines to show the inner part of the ear.

Sketch in more detail on the rat's head.

Add fingers to the paws.

Remember to give your rats expressions, just like humans! The positioning of the eye makes one rat look sneaky, but the other looks unsure.

Sketch in a line for the end of the tail.

Draw a small circle to show the rat's ankle bone.

Add toes to the rat's long rear paws.

Add tone to the drawing to give it more impact.

Use short, spiky lines for the rat's fur.

The use of light and dark to create bold, dramatic images is called chiaroscuro. Try this on your cartoon.

Make the edges of the body jagged to show the fur.

Add shade to the areas that face away from the light.

Draw lines across the rat's tail to complete it.

Remove any unwanted construction lines.

87

Bulldog

The bulldog is a classic cartoon character. Its face is perfect for a grumpy expression, which instantly gives it a character all of its own.

Mark in the positions of the ears and the nose.

The main shape of the bulldog is made with different-sized overlapping circles.

Draw a short line for the tail.

Body

Legs

Add short, curved lines for the legs.

Draw in the shape of the ears.

Add circles for the eyes, with straight lines above to make them look more aggressive.

Using the construction lines as a guide, add in the mouth and jowls.

Join the two circles of the body with straight lines.

Sketch in two curved lines for the neck and collar.

Add in the front legs and paws.

This foot is upturned, so you only see the sole. Sketch this in as a simple shape.

Add detail to the face.

Draw in the shape of the bulldog's back.

Draw more of the detail of the mouth and nose.

Finish the tail with curved lines.

Add small cones for the spikes on the collar.

Add areas of shade on the nose and around the eyes.

Add toes to the dog's paws.

Draw in the final details of the head.

Curved lines beside the legs give a feeling of movement.

Shade in areas around the collar and jowls.

Add shading to the underside of the bulldog.

Finish the paw of the bulldog with small circles.

Remove any unwanted construction lines.

DRAW Velociraptor

(ve-LOSS-e-rap-tor)

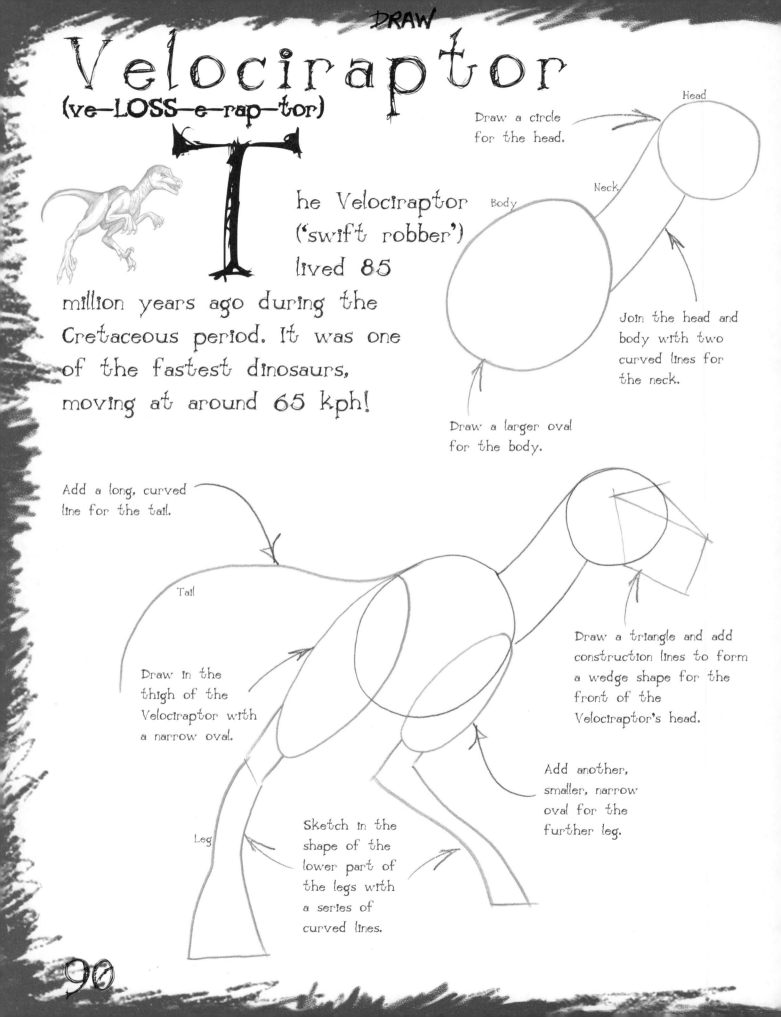

The Velociraptor ('swift robber') lived 85 million years ago during the Cretaceous period. It was one of the fastest dinosaurs, moving at around 65 kph!

Draw a circle for the head.

Head

Neck

Body

Join the head and body with two curved lines for the neck.

Draw a larger oval for the body.

Add a long, curved line for the tail.

Tail

Draw in the thigh of the Velociraptor with a narrow oval.

Leg

Sketch in the shape of the lower part of the legs with a series of curved lines.

Draw a triangle and add construction lines to form a wedge shape for the front of the Velociraptor's head.

Add another, smaller, narrow oval for the further leg.

Add a long, curved line for the underside of the tail, continuing it to complete the underside of the body.

Use the wedge—shaped construction lines to sketch in the face.

Each arm is made up of three circular joints, joined up with simple lines.

Sketch in the shape of the toes.

Talon

Add talons to the ends of the toes.

Add shading along the back of the Velociraptor.

Use your oval construction lines to draw the shape of the thigh and leg.

Complete the head, drawing the detail of the eyes and adding teeth.

Small lines can be added to give texture, such as wrinkles, to the skin.

Add shading and detail to the feet.

Using the construction lines, complete the hands, adding three talons to each.

Tyrannosaurus rex

(tie–RAN–o–sore–us REX)

At 5 tonnes and 12 metres in length, Tyrannosaurus rex ('tyrant lizard king') was one of the biggest theropods of all time. It was alive 85 million years ago in the Cretaceous period. The massive jaws and teeth provided an awesome biting force.

Above the body, draw a circle for the head, and two lines to form the neck. The line for the rear of the neck should miss the head slightly, then curve in.

Head

Neck

Body

Draw a large oval for the body.

Sketch in the construction lines for the head.

Position the arms by drawing ovals for the chest and a circle for the beginning of each arm.

Draw in the tail using two curved lines joining at the tip.

Tail

Draw a line from the chest down to the legs to complete the body shape.

Draw a narrow oval for the top of the hind leg.

Legs

Sketch in the legs using straight lines.

Using the construction lines, draw in the main details of the head. Include the nostrils, mouth and teeth.

Use the construction line midway through the head to mark the top of the mouth.

Draw circles on the construction lines for the elbow and wrist, joining them with straight lines.

The hand is a basic shape consisting of four lines.

Add a circle for the lower joint of the knee.

Use straight lines to complete the legs, with three pointed toes.

Use the construction lines to help you define the shape of the dinosaur's body.

Complete the detail on the head.

Add dark shading to the back for a chiaroscuro effect.

Draw many lines on the dinosaur's skin to give it texture.

Try some chiaroscuro (light and dark) on your dinosaur to get more impact.

Finish the details of the feet, adding talons.

Glossary

Chiaroscuro The practice of drawing high-contrast pictures with a lot of black and white, but not much grey.

Composition The arrangement of the parts of a picture on the drawing paper.

Construction lines Guidelines used in the early stages of a drawing. They are usually erased later.

Fixative A type of resin used to spray over a finished drawing to prevent smudging. **It should only be used by an adult.**

Focal point A central point of interest.

Foreshortening Drawing part of a figure shorter than it really is, so it looks as though it is pointing towards the viewer.

Light source The direction from which the light seems to come in a drawing.

Perspective A method of drawing in which near objects are shown larger than faraway objects to give an impression of depth.

Pose The position assumed by a figure.

Proportion The correct relationship of scale between each part of the drawing.

Silhouette A drawing that shows only a flat, dark shape, like a shadow.

Three-dimensional Having an effect of depth, so as to look lifelike or real.

Vanishing point The place in a perspective drawing where parallel lines appear to meet.

Index